Facts About the Walking Stick Insect
By Lisa Strattin
© 2016 Lisa Strattin
Revised 2022 © Lisa Strattin

FREE BOOK

FREE FOR ALL SUBSCRIBERS

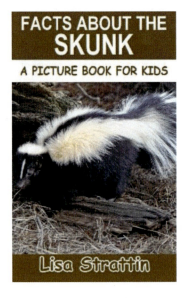

LisaStrattin.com/Subscribe-Here

BOX SET

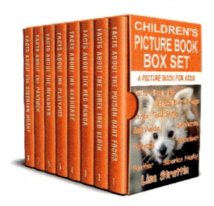

- **FACTS ABOUT THE POISON DART FROGS**
- **FACTS ABOUT THE THREE TOED SLOTH**
  - **FACTS ABOUT THE RED PANDA**
  - **FACTS ABOUT THE SEAHORSE**
  - **FACTS ABOUT THE PLATYPUS**
  - **FACTS ABOUT THE REINDEER**
  - **FACTS ABOUT THE PANTHER**
- **FACTS ABOUT THE SIBERIAN HUSKY**

LisaStrattin.com/BookBundle

Facts for Kids Picture Books by Lisa Strattin

Little Blue Penguin, Vol 92

Chipmunk, Vol 5

Frilled Lizard, Vol 39

Blue and Gold Macaw, Vol 13

Poison Dart Frogs, Vol 50

Blue Tarantula, Vol 115

African Elephants, Vol 8

Amur Leopard, Vol 89

Sabre Tooth Tiger, Vol 167

Baboon, Vol 174

Sign Up for New Release Emails Here

LisaStrattin.com/subscribe-here

All rights reserved. No part of this book may be reproduced by any means whatsoever without the written permission from the author, except brief portions quoted for purpose of review.

All information in this book has been carefully researched and checked for factual accuracy. However, the author and publisher makes no warranty, express or implied, that the information contained herein is appropriate for every individual, situation or purpose and assume no responsibility for errors or omissions. The reader assumes the risk and full responsibility for all actions, and the author will not be held responsible for any loss or damage, whether consequential, incidental, special or otherwise, that may result from the information presented in this book.

All images are free for use or purchased from stock photo sites or royalty free for commercial use.

Some coloring pages might be of the general species due to lack of available images.

I have relied on my own observations as well as many different sources for this book and I have done my best to check facts and give credit where it is due. In the event that any material is used without proper permission, please contact me so that the oversight can be corrected.

COVER IMAGE

https://www.flickr.com/photos/jsjgeology/19715518238/

ADDITIONAL IMAGES

https://www.flickr.com/photos/joos-gallery/51686742134/

https://www.flickr.com/photos/yokohamayomama/5764397547/

https://www.flickr.com/photos/whitesandsnps/29492672824/

https://www.flickr.com/photos/robandstephanielevy/3207433288/

https://www.flickr.com/photos/robandstephanielevy/3207432836/

https://www.flickr.com/photos/berniedup/6888582684/

https://www.flickr.com/photos/tristarada/3070519335/

https://www.flickr.com/photos/ahuett/2823923102/

https://www.flickr.com/photos/joos-gallery/51686739204/

https://www.flickr.com/photos/aecole/15323795629/

Contents

INTRODUCTION 9

CHARACTERISTICS 11

APPEARANCE 13

LIFE STAGES 15

LIFE SPAN 17

SIZE 19

HABITAT 21

DIET 23

FRIENDS AND ENEMIES 25

SUITABILITY AS PETS 27

INTRODUCTION

Walking Stick Insects look like sticks! They can be found world-wide with the exception of Antarctica, and they are most common in tropical regions. They vary in shape and color and have very good camouflage to avoid predators.

These insects eat leaves of trees and shrubs. They are known to remove most of the leaves on the trees in areas where there are high numbers of the insects. In some cases, entire stands of trees can have their leaves completely removed.

Walking Stick Insects have many nicknames because of their shape and color. In Europe, they are called *Stick Insects* and in the United States they are usually called *Stick Bugs* or *Walking Sticks*. Some people even call them *Ghost Insects* because of their ability to appear and disappear into their surroundings.

CHARACTERISTICS

Walking Sticks are usually long, slender insects that resemble sticks, but some have more flattened bodies and look just like leaves. These features help camouflage the insect from enemies. Most do not have wings, but some species do, and they use them to help escape. They are also very good at mimicry and will hang off a branch and sway back and forth to look like a twig blowing in the wind.

Walking Sticks, like other insects, have six legs. Each leg has two special pads. One of these pads is used for gripping and hanging on to trees, called sticky pads. They also have pads on their heels that are called non-sticky pads and they use them to help them lift the sticky pads in order to walk. If a predator grabs a walking stick by the leg, the leg will break off and then grow back in a few weeks!

APPEARANCE

Walking Sticks come in a variation of shapes, sizes and colors. In the United States, the most common insects are brown to green in color. Their bodies are long, thin, and rounded and they look like sticks and twigs. They have a great ability to camouflage themselves and are very hard to find in the wild. Even the eggs of walking sticks are camouflaged and resemble seeds.

They have long antennae that are 2/3 the length of their body. Males and females differ slightly in appearance. Males have light bands of color around their legs and females do not. Males also tend to be brown, while females are green in the ones native to the United States.

LIFE STAGES

Walking Sticks have three life stages. The first life stage is the egg. The females will lay their eggs almost anywhere, depending on the species. Some lay them in holes they dig and other will lay them on a plant. In total, a female Walking Stick can lay up to 1,200 eggs at a time! These eggs hatch within 20 to 30 days of being laid.

When the eggs hatch the Walking Sticks enter into the second life stage called the *nymph stage*. During this stage the insect will mature and develop toward adulthood. It can take several months for the insect to become an adult. The adult stage is the final stage.

LIFE SPAN

Walking Sticks reach adulthood in three months to one year and can live up to two years.

SIZE

Walking Sticks vary in size. They are as small as one inch and as long as 20 inches! Some walking sticks in Texas have been measured over seven inches long and may be the longest insects in the United States.

The eggs of a walking stick are about the size of small seeds.

HABITAT

Walking Sticks live in several habitats. These range from tropical rain forests in South America and Asia to the southwestern desert in the United States. These insects usually live on trees and bushes where they can hide.

In the southwestern United States, they are found primarily on creosote bushes. In the Midwestern and Eastern United States, they are often found on oak, cherry, and hazel trees.

DIET

Walking Sticks primarily eat the leaves of trees and shrubs. They usually feed at night and can eat all of the leaves off of stands of trees in a short time.

In the southwestern United States, they feed on creosote bushes, and in the eastern United States, they feed on oak and locust trees. When a Walking Stick feeds they do not eat the entire leaf but just the fleshy parts between the veins and stem.

FRIENDS AND ENEMIES

Walking Sticks like to live in groups with other Walking Stick Insects. They do not have any other friends.

Birds, bats, and monkeys are all enemies. These animals will all look for and attack these insects if they can find them. They have a few tricks to avoid being attacked. Since they feed primarily at night, they use their color and shape as camouflage when resting during the day. Their color and stick shape helps them to blend into their tree and shrub habitat easily.

Some kinds of Walking Sticks have brightly colored wings they will flash at an animal to scare it off. In some cases, lichens (a plant) will grow on a Walking Stick and helps it hide in the habitat. The Walking Stick species in the eastern United States releases a foul smelling and tasting substance to deter animals from investigating it too closely.

SUITABILITY AS PETS

Walking Sticks have been kept as pets. Many of these species have been raised in laboratories so that researchers can study the way they walk. A Walking Stick from India is commonly kept as a pet because it readily eats vegetables and is easy to keep alive.

In the United States, as of this writing, only the Northern Walking Stick is legal to own as a pet, but they are very hard to keep alive because they require a diverse diet.

COLOR ME

COLOR ME

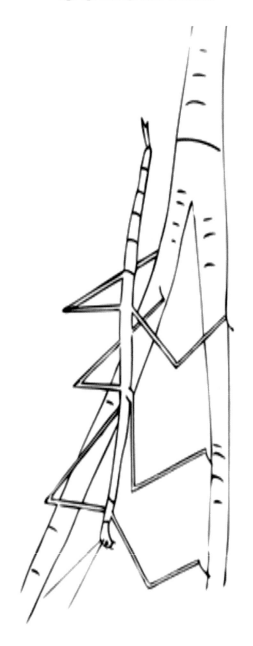

COLOR ME

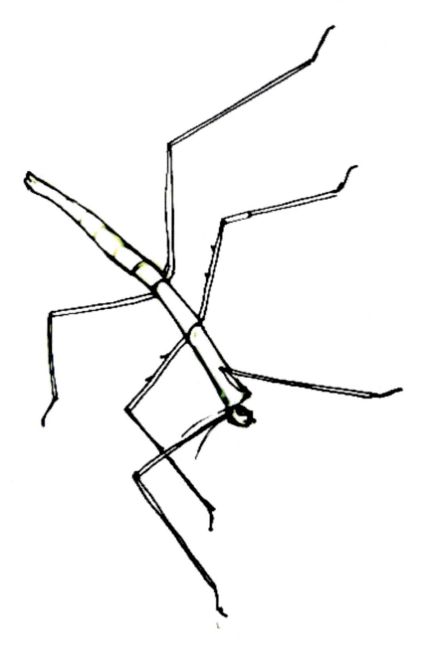

COLOR ME

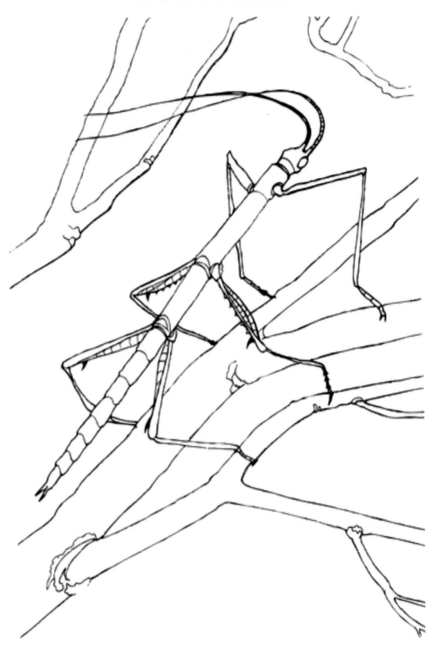

COLOR ME

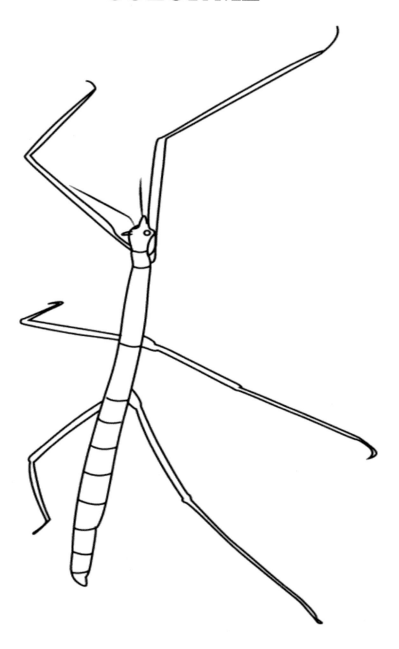

COLOR ME

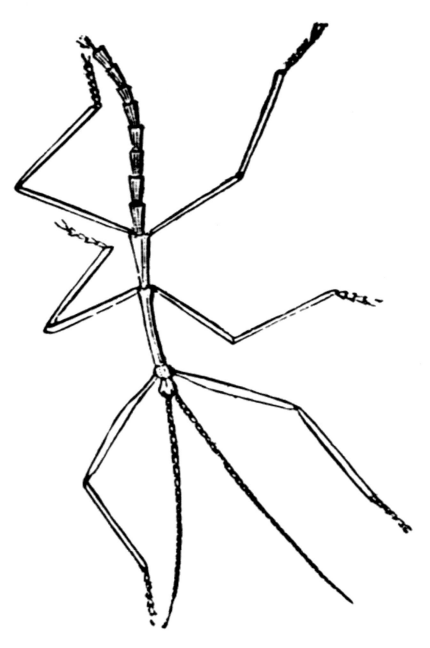

COLOR ME

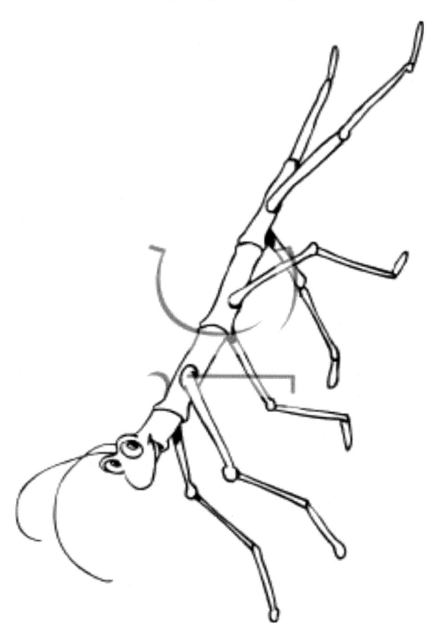

COLOR ME

COLOR ME

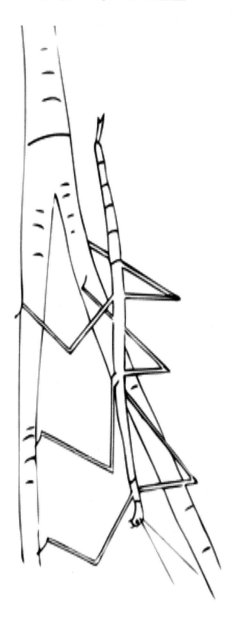

COLOR ME

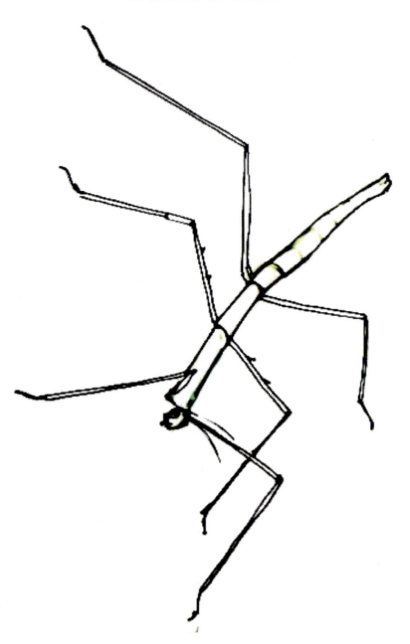

Please leave me a review here:

Lisastrattin.com/Review-Vol-80

For more Kindle Downloads Visit Lisa Strattin Author Page on Amazon Author Central

amazon.com/author/lisastrattin

To see upcoming titles, visit my website at LisaStrattin.com– most books available on Kindle!

LisaStrattin.com

FREE BOOK

FOR ALL SUBSCRIBERS – SIGN UP NOW

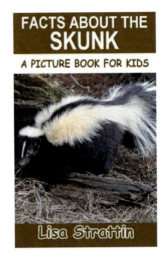

LisaStrattin.com/Subscribe-Here

LisaStrattin.com/Facebook

LisaStrattin.com/Youtube

Made in the USA
Las Vegas, NV
11 January 2024